Romans:
Made Righteous by Faith

Gladys Hunt

14 inductive studies
for neighborhood,
student and
church groups

Harold Shaw Publishers
Wheaton, Illinois

ISBN 0-87788-733-0

Printed in the United States of America

92 91 90 89 88 87 86 85 84 83 82 81

10 9 8 7 6 5 4 3 2

Contents

INTRODUCTION

THE STUDY OF ROMANS

As you study the letter to the *Romans,* Paul's profound explanation of the Gospel of Jesus Christ, you will find abundant treasures! William Tyndale, who was martyred for his efforts to translate the Bible into the language of the people, wrote in his prologue to *Romans* that it was a book of "glad tidings and a light and a way into the whole scripture. . . . No man verily can read it too oft or study it too well: for the more it is studied the easier it is, the more it is chewed the pleasanter it is, and the more groundly it is searched the preciouser things are found in it, so great of spiritual things lieth hid therein."

The themes of this letter are basic to Christianity. The ideas represented by words like Law, Sin, Grace, Faith, Righteousness, Flesh, Spirit are keys to understanding what the Gospel is about. Paul is answering the question, "How can sinful man be made right with God?" From the sweeping wrath of God against sin to the overwhelming grace of God in Christ Jesus, Paul explains God's way to righteousness by faith in Chapters 1-5. Romans 3:24 stands alongside John 3:16 as a magnificent capsule of Good News: "They are justified by his grace as a gift, through the redemption which is in Christ Jesus."

In Chapters 6-8 Paul adds to this Good News the liberating secret to living a holy life. What the law could not do, grace does. Chapters 9-11 are a parenthetical discussion about Jewish unbelief and the purpose of God. In Chapters 12-15 Paul fairly shouts with triumph about the practical outworkings of redemption in daily life.

Romans is a meaty, challenging letter from start to finish. You won't be the same after studying it.

PREPARE TO BE CHANGED

Paul's teaching in *Romans* has challenged the lives of those who have led the Christian church in more ways than can be recounted.

We do know, for instance, that the light which the Holy Spirit used to illumine the mind of Augustine in A.D. 386 was Romans 13:13, 14. The details of this are found in Study 12.

In 1515 Martin Luther, an Augustinian monk, began to expound the Roman letter to his students. One expression from the letter stood in the way of his understanding. It was *"the righteousness of God."* He writes, "Night and day I pondered until . . . I grasped the truth that the righteousness of God is that righteousness whereby, through grace and sheer mercy, he justifies us by faith. Thereupon I felt myself to be reborn and to have gone through open doors into paradise" (Luther's Works, Vol. 54, Weimar edition, p. 179).

In May 1738 John Wesley went to a meeting in Aldersgate Street where someone was reading Luther's Preface to the Epistle to the Romans. He later wrote in his journal, "While he [Luther] was describing the change which God works in the heart through faith in Christ, I felt myself strangely warmed. I felt I did trust in Christ, Christ alone, for my salvation; and an assurance was given me that he had taken *my* sins away, even *mine;* and saved me from the law of sin and death" (*Works,* Vol. I, 1872, p. 103). He said about his conversion, "I exchanged the faith of a servant for the faith of a son."

In 1534 William Tyndale wrote this admonition about *Romans:*
"Now go to, reader, and according to the order of Paul's writing, even so do thou. First behold thyself diligently in the law of God, and see there thy just damnation. Secondarily, turn thine eyes to Christ, and see there the exceeding mercy of thy most kind and loving Father. Thirdly, remember that Christ made not this atonement that thou shouldest anger God again: neither cleansed he thee, that thou shouldest return (as a swine) unto thine old puddle again: but that thou sholdest be a new creature and live a new life after the will of God and not of the flesh."

THE BACKGROUND OF THE LETTER TO THE ROMANS
This is Paul's last letter before his prolonged imprisonment which followed the visit to Jerusalem he mentions in Romans 15.

Paul dreamed of going to Rome to preach in that great city. (See Acts 19:21, Acts 23:11 and Romans 1:15.) He was in Corinth sometime in the year A.D. 58 when he wrote to the Roman church. His plan was to return to the church at Jerusalem, bringing a collection from the younger churches as a practical demonstration of the unity and care within the body of believers, and then go on to Rome.

But Paul had more in mind than going to Rome. As a master strategist, he wanted to take the Gospel to Spain, the end of the then-known-world. Rome would be his base of operation. This letter to the Romans contains both his splendid treatise on the Gospel and an explanation of his missionary purpose.

THE OUTLINE OF THE BOOK

Romans   1-5 The way to righteousness
            6-8 The way to holiness
          9-11 The problem of unbelief and the Jews
       12-15 Practical Christian living
          16 Personal greetings and benediction

HOW SHOULD IT BE STUDIED?

This study of *Romans* is designed for small group discussion as an inductive study. It can be used in personal study as well. In a group, each member should have a copy of the studyguide. The group will benefit most if each member studies the material independently before they meet.

However, remember the studyguide is the teacher only in the sense that it drives group members into the text of the Scripture to see what it really says. It is there that the Holy Spirit is the Real Teacher. Do not study the guide; study the Bible.

The leadership of the study may be rotated, but the discussion leader will want to prepare thoroughly before the group meets. The leader should be familiar enough with the text and the direction of the discussion questions to guide the discussion along and keep the study on target. He is not the answer man; he only fields the questions to the group. The answers are in the text.

The group members participate in discovering what the text is saying by using the discussion questions and by making additional observations of their own. What is personally discovered is always more one's own than what is taught in lecture form.

The leader must be careful not to talk too much. The traffic pattern of group contribution should not be from leader to group member and then back to leader but discussion should move naturally among group members. Allow time for group discussion. If you wait, others will share their thoughts, particularly on interpretation and application questions. When the leader rushes from question to question, keeping too tight a rein on discussion, the group tends to become rigid and mechanical—a kind of question and answer time, rather than a discussion.

The leader can encourage less talkative members by eye-contact, by waiting a reasonable amount of time, or by asking an opinion question in a sensitive way. If someone is always quick to give an answer, reassure the group by asking, "What do the rest of you think?"

Space is provided between questions for jotting down answers and personal notations as a learning help, not as a fill-in-the-blank technique.

The discussion questions will fall into three categories:
What does it say?/ FIND THE FACTS
What does it mean?/ INTERPRET
What does it mean to me?/ APPLY
Make certain that you get the facts before you begin to interpret. The facts excite the interpretation and the application.

FOR THE DISCUSSION LEADER

1. The grouping of questions is based on the paragraphing found in the Revised Standard Version and the New International Version. Question wording is also based on the wording of the R.S.V., and N.I.V., although most modern translations of the Bible may be used in the study. Unless other instructions are given, each section should be read aloud to the group before they discuss together the questions in the guide.

2. Questions are numbered to denote topics of discussion. *Read only one question in the series at a time.* Move on quickly through the series as each question is completed.

3. Any note or quotation which helps illumine the text *should be read after* the group's discussion of the preceding questions.

4. When references to verses elsewhere in the Bible are given in the study-guide, it may speed the flow of discussion if the leader writes these references on slips of paper and distributes them to group members before the study, to be read when called for.

5. Keep a careful check on the time. Begin and end the study at the agreed hour.

6. Your job is to keep the group on target. The target is the Bible passage being studied. Keep the study moving along so that you can complete the assigned lesson.

7. Each study contains background facts which build up to the major point of the passage. The leader needs to be sufficiently familiar with the material to apportion available time wisely. Otherwise the most significant part of the passage may not have adequate discussion time.

8. If you find the study material too long, adjust carefully according to subject and paragraphing. However, beware of dawdling through a study. Covering too little material discourages most people.

9. Encourage everyone to participate in the discussion. Stress that the answers to the discussion questions lie in the text. If a member contributes an idea that seems irrelevant, it is appropriate to ask openly, "Which verse suggests that idea to you?"

10. Tangents can be time consuming. Unless they are relevant to the discussion, suggest tabling any tangents and discussing them later.

11. Pray that God will make the group congenial, and open minded—and that he will be the real teacher as you discuss the Bible together.

DISCUSSION RULES FOR GROUP MEMBERS

Agree ahead of time to follow the rules of good discussion. If new members join the study after you have started, review the rules for the whole group.

1. Stick to the chapter being studied. Don't jump around in the Bible, looking up verses or passages that come to your mind. Let this passage speak for itself. If it needs additional background, the guide will give the references. This rule saves the group from confusion and insecurity.

2. However, as the study continues it will be natural and helpful to refer back to earlier sections in *Romans* because then the group will have a common frame of reference.

3. Try to avoid tangents. Group members can get off on long discourses about personal hangups or ideas they have heard before—often subjects which lead away from the main point of the study. Remind each other to stick to the passage.

4. Encourage each one to take part. Group members can do this by being sensitive to the needs of the study. Some will need to discipline themselves to speak less, others to speak more.

5. The discussion leaders will ask for volunteers to read. Some people simply don't like reading aloud. If you include prayer (which is a good idea) always ask someone ahead of time. Avoid surprises which might lead to embarrassment!

6. Expect God to teach you more than you've learned before. You will not understand everything in *Romans*. Don't let that discourage you. Learn from what you do understand and the Holy Spirit will give you increasing insights into what is important.

7. Let the document be the authority—not someone's interpretation or what they *think* the passage says. For this reason use a modern translation of the Bible in this study, rather than a paraphrase.

1

GOD'S RIGHTEOUSNESS AND WRATH

ROMANS 1

What an introduction! Notice the breadth of range in the content packed into the first seventeen verses. Remember, Paul had never been to Rome, though he had met a number of members of the Roman congregation elsewhere during his travels. Think how you would describe Paul if this passage were your only source of information about him.

In this chapter Paul makes a strong statement about the power of the Gospel, God's way to righteousness, in verses 16 and 17. But before he elaborates on the Gospel he needs to show how desperately mankind needs the mercy and pardon of God. Verses 18-32 begin a vivid description of the pagans of Paul's time.

Romans 1:1-17

Read these verses aloud.
1/How does Paul identify himself in these verses? Compare Galatians 1:15, 16. How would you identify yourself if *you* were writing to an unknown audience? Why?

_____

_____

_____

_____

2/Paul summarizes the Gospel in verses 1-5. Discuss:
a/What is its origin? _____
b/How has it been made known? _____
c/Who is its central focus? _____

d/For whom is it given? _____

e/For what purpose? _____

f/For whose sake, ultimately? _____

g/How is Paul involved in it? _____

Discuss the meaning of the phrase "the obedience of faith" (verse 5).

_____

_____

3/From verses 3-5, what do we learn about Jesus?

_____

_____

4/How does Paul describe the people to whom he is writing (verses 6-8)? What is his relationship with them (verses 8-13)?

_____

_____

_____

note: "loved by God," "called to belong," "called to be saints:" all these phrases are in the passive voice, indicating that God took the initiative in reaching out to those who became his people in Rome and, by implication, to people in any age—to us!

5/What are Paul's three reasons for wanting to go to Rome (verses 12, 13)? What three statements about himself show Paul's zeal and commitment (verses 14-16)? Discuss the implications of these ideas in your own life (i.e., Are you under obligation, a "debtor?" Why? Are you eager? For what? Why? Are you ashamed of the Gospel? Why? If not, why not?).

_____

_____

_____

_____

_____

6/What does Paul believe about the Gospel (verses 16, 17)? How does this relate to his zeal?

note: "The righteousness of God revealed" is one definition of the Gospel. Keep this in mind as you study further.

Romans 1:18-32

Read these verses aloud.
7/Contrast the two things being revealed in verses 17 and 18. Against whom is God's wrath directed? Why?

8/On what basis is mankind without excuse? Trace man's downward steps to the appalling perversion of verse 23. In what variety of ways does man refuse to honor God? Is open rebellion the only way? Why is "giving thanks" important? What does thankfulness indicate in a relationship?

9/Why did God "give them up" or "let them go" (verses 24, 26, 28)? How is this evidence of God's wrath? What is wrath? Check your definition with what you know about the character of God. Does his wrath arise because of some other aspect of his character? If God is perfect holiness, how _must_ he react to unholiness?

_____

_____

_____

_____

note: God's wrath may be defined as his unchanging opposition to sin.

10/After reading this passage, how would you define *sin*? Note the variety of sins listed in verses 28-32. Look at each of them. In what ways are they similar? How do they differ? Why does Paul lump together such a diversity of sins? How would you answer someone who says that homosexuality is a valid expression of relationship? What happens when people leave God out of their thinking?

_____

_____

_____

_____

11/As defined in this passage, what attitude toward God characterizes sin? Explain. Note how verse 23 underscores this.

_____

12/By contrast, what characterizes the attitude with which a person comes into right relationship with God (verse 17)? What words help describe an attitude of faith? What is *your* attitude toward God?

_____

_____

_____

*note: C. S. Lewis observes that men who choose against God are left to "enjoy forever the horrible freedom they have demanded and are therefore self-enslaved" (*The Problem of Pain, Macmillan Publishing Co., Inc., p. 115*).*

CONCLUSION

As you close, thank God that his way to righteousness makes up for all the inadequacies of sinful people in a needy world. Ask God to help you to be like Paul in those areas in which you would like to imitate him.

2

GUILTY BEFORE GOD

ROMANS 2—3:20

Paul imagines the readers' responses to his shattering description of pagan
lostness in Chapter 1. He can hear their protests of innocence and see them
console themselves with thoughts of their own morality. The Jews, especially,
thought that they occupied a privileged position before God. But Paul does not
pull his punches. Each of us, he emphasizes, is guilty before God.

Romans 2:1-16

Read these verses aloud.
1/The list of perversities in 1:18-32 may prompt a self-righteous response in
readers: "Well . . . others may act like that, but not me." What does Paul say
to such moralists in 2:1-4? Of what does he accuse them? How has the kindness, forbearance and patience of God (verse 4) affected your life? Has it led
you to complacency or holiness? Can God's wrath (as defined in the previous
study) be seen as an expression of God's kindness?

_____

_____

_____

_____

_____

2/How does the attitude of those in 2:3 resemble the attitude of the pagans
in 1:18-32? What does an unrepentant heart say about a person's relationship
to God (verses 4, 5)? What is the point of Paul's discussion about works in
verses 6-11? Is he saying that works "save" anyone? What is the result of
choosing evil? good? In verses 9, 10, who had the advantage, Jew or Greek?
Why?

_____

_____

_____

_____

_____

_____

3/What can be learned about God's judgment in 2:1-16? Find at least six ideas. By what standard will the Gentiles be judged? the Jews? According to verses 14, 15, why are people who have never been taught God's law still accountable to him? Do you always live up to the standard set by your conscience?

_____

_____

_____

_____

_____

note: "Though God justifies us by faith, he will judge us by our works. For the day of judgment will be a public occasion, and will require public evidence. This principle applies equally to Jews and Gentiles. For both know God's moral law, though in different ways" (John R. W. Stott, Urbana, 1979).

Romans 2:17-29

Read these verses aloud.
4/How do "religious" people fool themselves? Why is knowledge not enough? What dishonor do "religious" people bring to God's name? What had happened to the Jewish people over a period of time? How does this still happen in organized Christianity?

_____

_____

5/According to verses 25-29, in what were the Jews trusting to make them-selves acceptable to God? What kind of circumcision is God really looking for? (Compare Deuteronomy 10:16 and Jeremiah 9:25, 26.) What outward symbols or actions make you feel religious but might keep you from spiritual reality? How does Paul describe "a real Jew?" Are you one? How did it happen?

Romans 3:1-20

Read these verses aloud.
6/What anticipated objections from Jewish readers does Paul answer here? (Give both the questions and the answers.) Summarize the argument of verses 5-8. Why do we try to justify our sins?

7/What does Paul conclude about humanity? What words emphasize the universality of sin in verses 10-12? What parts of the body are involved in sin? What words describe the results of evil conduct?

_____

_____

8/Why can a person never become completely righteous by doing good (keeping the law)? What, then, is the purpose of God's law? How might a consciousness of our sin lead us to God? Compare Galatians 3:21-25.

_____

_____

_____

note: Romans 3:10-17 presents a series of Old Testament quotations. Human beings are undone before God; they are depraved, to use a theological word. That does not mean that we are all as bad as we can be. The truth is that we are not as good as we should be to meet the standards of a holy God.

9/Review question: In his judgment of humans, does God consider whether a person is a respectable, "high class" sinner or an ignorant, pagan murderer? What verses support your answer?

_____

_____

10/Verses 19, 20 summarize Paul's whole argument thus far. Paraphrase his ideas in your own words.

_____

_____

_____

CONCLUSION

Admitting that you are guilty before God is difficult only if you have no solution to the problem of sin or you feel obligated to provide your own righteousness by good works. Look ahead to the next study and read Romans 3:21-24. This is the "Gospel of righteousness from God" that Paul wrote about in 1:17. After we examine our own hearts we are forced to say yes to 3:10. That honest admission also leads us to embrace with joy the good news that Jesus makes people righteous through faith.

Close your session together by thanking God for providing you with insight and understanding through his Word and his Spirit.

3

GOD'S GOOD NEWS

ROMANS 3:21—4:25

Now Paul speaks with a new note of optimism; he turns from the unrighteousness of humanity to the righteousness of God. Compare 1:18 with 3:21 and note the burst of hope in the words *"but now...."* This righteousness from God is the divine solution to the problem: how can evil human beings become pure and holy? This can be defined as *God's justifying grace.* In Romans 4, Paul shows how the principle of God's justifying grace was demonstrated in Abraham's life. This study answers the key question: how can sinful people move into a right relationship with God?

Suggestion: Memorize Romans 3:24 and John 3:16; both verses capsulize the Good News in different ways.

Reminder: Do not read or discuss any *note* given in a study until *after* the group has discussed the question to which it refers.

Romans 3:21-31

Read these verses aloud around the group.
1/What do these verses say about God's righteousness? Note the prepositions in verse 22. Note also who are the principals involved in this process of sinful man being made righteous by faith. Who takes the initiative?

_____

_____

_____

2/Who needs this righteousness from God? What does it mean to "fall short of the glory of God?" From your own experience, give an example of how you "fell short" in the performance of some duty or responsibility. What did you feel? If you have felt inadequate in fulfilling a human obligation, how do you feel when you fail God?

_____

_____

_____

note: The word Paul uses here for falling short is the same word that Jesus used in the Parable of the Prodigal Son (Luke 15:11-32), when he said that the young man began "to be in want." When we are in want of God's glory, what do we lack? Righteousness.

3/Check the definitions of justify and justification in a good dictionary. What happens when a person is justified? Compare verses 22 and 24. What does a person receive when he is justified? What did it cost? Who paid for it?

_____

_____

_____

4/What did the death of Jesus Christ demonstrate (verses 25, 26)? Why can't God overlook sin? What does this show you about his character?

_____

_____

5/Using a dictionary, define redemption (verse 24) and propitiation (or expiation, as in the RSV, verse 25). Discuss why both of these transactions are necessary in our rescue from sin. Who initiates both actions? Who benefits from both?

_____

_____

_____

_____

6/How may we participate in God's justifying grace? Note the repetition of faith and belief in these verses. Who is the object of our faith? When you are given something (verse 24), what action is necessary on your part? Have you taken that action?

_____

_____

_____

7/List the six questions of verses 27-31. As you analyze the answers to these questions, what principles can you identify in the process of justification? If acceptance by God came only through the Jewish law, what would happen to some of us?

_____

_____

_____

_____

_____

_____

note: Faith functions in three ways in verses 27-31: a) faith humbles the sinner and excludes boasting, b) faith unites the church and excludes discrimination, c) faith establishes the Scripture and excludes contradiction (John R. W. Stott, in an exposition of Romans, Urbana, 1979).

Romans 4

Read these verses aloud.
8/On what grounds was Abraham justified (declared righteous)? under what circumstances (verses 5, 10, 13)? Did Abraham have God's law? By implication, whose righteousness was he given? What is Paul's argument in using Abraham as an example (compare 3:21)? What does Paul's quotation from David in verses 6, 7 add to his argument? How does Abraham become our father (verse 16, 17)? How does this destroy all natural barriers and prejudice?

_____

_____

_____

_____

_____

_____

9/Note the word *reckoned* (or *credited to*) in verses 3 and 5. What does this mean? Discuss the cause and effect relationship: I believe God, therefore God credits Jesus' righteousness to my account. Give evidence from today's study that this is what the Scriptures teach. What has God said about your sin, his solution, your response?

_____

_____

_____

10/In 3:24 and 4:16, the word *grace* shines out from the page. What does grace mean, from the dictionary? What does it mean to you personally?

_____

_____

note: Grace may be defined by an acrostic:
G - God's
R - Riches
A - At
C - Christ's
E - Expense

11/*Believe* is another crucial word. How does the example of Abraham in verses 13-25 help you understand the biblical meaning of *believing*? What did Abraham believe about God?

_____

_____

note: If you are unfamiliar with the story of Abraham, read Genesis 15 and 17.

12/What has God said we must believe in order to be counted righteous?

Express the facts of 4:24, 25 in your own words as a summary of the Gospel.

_____

_____

(Discuss the following questions if you have time, or use them as a review.)

13/How would you answer the question: How can a sinful person be acceptable to a holy God?

_____

14/Why do most people find it easier to accept the idea of a works-righteousness rather than a faith-righteousness?

_____

15/Do you ever find yourself slipping into a belief in works-righteousness? Why?

_____

CONCLUSION

Justification is one of the largest, most crucial concepts in the Bible. Here are some thoughts on its meaning from D. Martyn Lloyd-Jones in his exposition of *Romans* (pp. 54 ff., Zondervan). "Justification makes no actual change in us; it is a declaration by God concerning us. It is not something that results from what we do but rather something that is done to us. . . . We are declared righteous the moment we exercise faith. . . . It comes to us freely and by the grace of God; it is a free gift to those who deserve the exact opposite. This great doctrine of justification teaches us that God not only forgives us but also puts to our account the righteousness of Jesus Christ."

Would your life be different if you awoke every morning with a fresh sense that "I have been declared righteous by God through faith in Jesus?" Try it!

4

MADE RIGHT WITH GOD

(This study may be divided in two, if desired.)

ROMANS 5

As a test of what was learned last week, ask the group the following questions:

a. Which of the following two statements is wholly true?

God in his mercy and grace finds me a sinner and through my faith he begins to develop me as a new creation in Christian character and righteousness. That righteousness allows me to stand before God both now and in the day of judgment, justified by faith.

God in his mercy and grace finds me a sinner and gives me the righteousness of Jesus Christ, which I receive by faith. I am, therefore, able to stand before God now and in the day of judgment, justified by faith.

b. As I grow in my Christian life and become more mature, will my acceptance by God likewise grow, or is it settled today?

c. Does God accept me as his child and give me eternal life based on anything he sees in my life? If so, what?

Romans 5:1-5

Read these verses aloud.
1/In your own words, explain the meaning of the words "justified by faith" as you would to someone hearing this for the first time.

_____

_____

2/What three privileges belong to "justified ones" (verses 1-2)? Discuss the significance of each in your own life. How is peace *with* God different from the peace *of* God mentioned in Philippians 4:7? How have all these blessings become ours?

_____

_____

_____

note: The word "access" used in verse 2 is the regular word for introducing or ushering someone into the presence of royalty. "Jesus ushers us into the very presence of God. Jesus opens the door for us to the presence of the King of Kings; and when that door is opened what we find is grace; *not condemnation, not judgment, not vengeance, but the sheer, undeserved, unearned, unmerited, incredible kindness of God" (William Barclay,* Romans, *Westminster; p. 71).*

3/How is the unpleasantness of suffering changed for believers? What does this tell us about God's long-range plans and goals for us? Should Christians *expect* trial and suffering as a part of life? (Note Acts 14:22 and John 16:33.) Point out specific ways in which suffering or trial have helped you grow.

_____

_____

_____

note: "We must learn to view all human suffering and tragedy from the vantage ground of the cross" (J. R. W. Stott).

4/How would you define Christian hope? List the ways in which it is used in verses 1-5. Why is this hope so refreshing to our spirits? What is the ultimate focus of our hope? (See John 17:24 and Colossians 3:4.)

_____

_____

_____

5/What do you learn about the Holy Spirit's ministry from verse 5? What fruits of the Holy Spirit, listed in Galatians 5:22, appear in the first five verses of this chapter? Which of these fruits still need to grow in your life?

_____

Romans 5:6-11

Read these verses aloud.

6/What words describe our condition as sinners in these verses? How can we be *sure* God loves us? What other assurance of his personal love has already been mentioned in verse 5?

7/Define *reconciliation* (verses 10, 11). Follow Paul's argument in verse 9-11 to show how secure is the salvation of those who are justified.

note: *Justification changes our status; we are declared* righteous, *by faith. Reconciliation (the end of hostility, the moving together of two parties into renewed love and harmony) enables us to grow in our relationship with God so that we are in the* process *of "being saved" from our own isolation and inadequacy.*

8/Verse 11 encapsulates the wonder of the position of justified persons. In whom do we now rejoice? Through whom is this possible? What is our cause for rejoicing? Compare verse 11 with verse 3, then contrast this exultation and rejoicing with the boasting of 2:17.

9/Are you rejoicing? How does being reconciled and justified affect your view of yourself? of God? of Christ? What difference does this make in your interpersonal relationships? Compare *your* attitude with that described in verse 17.

Romans 5:12-21

Read these verses aloud around the group.
10/Make a list of all that this passage says about sin. How are sin and death related? sin and law? (Compare 2:12 and 3:19, 20.)

11/Trace Adam's action and its results. Contrast this with Christ's action and its results. What phrases are used to highlight the contrast? Use the chart below to record what you find.

Adam	*Christ*
sin entered	grace entered

12/Contrast the meaning of death's reign (verses 14, 17) with the believers' reign (verse 17). What difference does this make in your life? How do verses 20b and 21 add to your understanding of your position in Christ? What makes a "reigning life" or a "life of victory" possible?

13/Observe the *"much more"* arguments in this chapter (verses 9, 10, 15, 17). Notice that the first two (verses 9, 10) argue from the greater to the lesser and the second two (verses 15, 17) argue from the lesser to the greater. In both instances, what is Paul's conclusion?

_____

_____

14/List the times the preposition *through* is used in this chapter. What does this underscore about our redemption?

_____

_____

15/How much of the Gospel could you explain to someone by using Romans 5 alone? What would you particularly want to emphasize, based on your own experience of understanding God's plan.

_____

_____

_____

CONCLUSION

Whose righteousness do you count on—your own or Jesus'? Close with brief, sentence prayers thanking God for all that being made right with him means to you. Ask God to help you rejoice and reign through life with Jesus Christ!

5

DEAD—AND ALIVE!

ROMANS 6

This chapter is like a treasure chest; it opens up to us some of the most liberating, encouraging truths in the Bible. Verses 1-10 complete Paul's doctrinal statements about God's great plan in making men right with himself. Union with Christ releases a believer from the dominion, or enslavement, of sin.

The second part of the chapter helps us to work out the implications of this freedom; what does it mean to live a holy life in the light of these great truths? Paul speaks it out clearly: Don't allow sin to master you in any part of your life! You are dead to sin, now, and alive to God. As believers, each of us has a new life within us; *Christ dwells in us!* We have the power within us, then, to resist the seduction of sin.

Romans 6:1-14

Read these verses aloud.
1/Refer back to Romans 5:20. What wrong conclusion could come from a misapplication of the last half of this verse? Compare Romans 3:8. Paul sees the problem coming and heads it off. How does he handle this possible argument? How do people today (yourself included) make God's mercy an excuse for sinning? Think of specific examples.

_____

_____

_____

note: A cheap misuse of the grace of God is such a selfish exploitation of God's plan that the church has often created its own set of rules to prevent such abuse. In Paul's day some people wanted to impose an obligatory adherence to the Law of Moses as a condition of salvation, in addition to faith

34

in Christ. Paul goes on to explain that God's provision for a holy life is union with Christ, not legalism.

2/When a person believes in Jesus Christ, some radical changes take place. Using the ideas in Ephesians 2:1-6, I Corinthians 12:13 and Galatians 2:20, write a summary statement that describes this life-changing transaction between a person and God.

_____

_____

_____

3/In what two contrasting ways are believers identified with Christ (Romans 6:4, 5, 8)? Is the baptism of verses 3 and 4 primarily a physical or a spiritual experience? Give reasons for your answer.

_____

_____

_____

note: The Christian ordinance of baptism is a symbol of what has already happened to a person when he believed (committed his life to) Jesus Christ. (Compare Acts 8:26-39.) The baptism here referred to is the mystical action of the Holy Spirit of God who joins us to Christ. It is he who "puts us into" the body of Christ, the family of God.

4/From verses 4-10, list some of the implications or results of being united with Christ in his death. Now list the results of being united with Christ in his resurrection. Do these results belong to the present or the future?

_____

_____

_____

5/What does it mean to be "dead to sin?" Refer to the list you made in answer to question 11 of Study 4. What is the status of a person *in Adam?* What is the status of a person who is *in Christ?* If you have trusted your life to Christ as your Savior, are you now in Adam or in Christ, with regard to your sin? Does this mean that a Christian is sinless? What freedom do we have? On what basis?

_____

_____

_____

_____

_____

6/Verse 11 is a turning point in this letter from Paul. Now he begins to apply the truths he has been presenting. What instructions does he give in verses 11-14? List both their negative and positive aspects. What key words can you identify?

_____

_____

_____

7/What foundational truth makes it possible for believers to obey these instructions? Give practical examples from your own life of how identification or union with Christ has affected your choices, your discipline, your personal holiness.

_____

_____

_____

8/How would you explain to someone who doesn't know God what it is like to be "alive to God" (verse 11)? How should being alive to God change your attitude toward yourself? What confidence should this truth give you about future events? How should it affect your attitude toward sin?

_____

_____

_____

Romans 6:15-23

Read these verses aloud around the group.

9/Compare Paul's question in verse 15 with that of verse 1. How does he expand his reasoning about the absurdity of such an idea? Why do you think he uses the analogy of slavery? How can you know whose slave you are (verse 16)? According to verse 18, what freedom do believers have?

_____

_____

_____

_____

10/Compare the benefits of sin with the benefits of obedience. What is the end result of each? Note the two sets of opposites in verse 23. Identify them and discuss what is earned and what is given. (Compare 5:21 and 3:24.) Why can there be no middle ground in the matter of whom you obey?

_____

_____

_____

CONCLUSION

Summarize the principle of identification with Christ (verses 1-10) and how this identification helps you live a holy life (verses 11-23). Close with sentence prayers, thanking God for freeing you from slavery to sin and for making you free, and alive to God. Write out verse 11 and post it where you can see and read it often during the next week.

6

NOT I, BUT CHRIST

ROMANS 7

In Chapters 6 and 7 Paul answers an imaginary inquirer who might ask, "If I am justified freely as a gift of God by faith, what should be my attitude toward sin and God's law? I understand that grace sets me free from sin's power. But what should I do about keeping the law?"

In Chapter 6 Paul emphasizes that faith places us "in Christ" and thus we are identified with him, even with his death and resurrection. We died to sin; we are alive to God. Now, in Chapter 7, he brings up the question of the law and speaks from the experience of his own past efforts to be righteous by keeping the law. He wants his readers to understand clearly that legalism ("law-keeping") is *not* the way to righteousness. He has made this point before, in 3:20 and 6:14; now he develops it more fully.

Romans 7

Read these verses aloud.
1/What basic truth is Paul illustrating by using the marriage analogy in verses 1-3?

_____

_____

2/Who has died, according to verses 4-6? What bond has been broken? What evidence of identification with Christ (as introduced in Chapter 6) do you see in this paragraph?

_____

_____

3/What effect did the law have on behavior and holiness (verse 5)? Contrast this with the effects of the new life in Christ. Compare 2 Corinthians 3:6.

_____

_____

_____

note: We need to realize that the new relationship (verse 4) cannot be broken by death. Compare Romans 6:9.

4/What good purpose did the law fulfill (verse 7)? What commandment does Paul single out as a primary human problem? Compare Colossians 3:5. How does this relate to the Fall in the Garden of Eden (Romans 7:11)? •

_____

_____

_____

5/Explain the meaning of the statement: "Apart from the law, sin is dead" (verse 8b and 9a). Does the law indeed create sin? Where does the problem lie? Illustrate from your own life how a prohibition aroused your desire for a forbidden act or thing.

_____

_____

_____

6/What conclusions (verse 12) does Paul make about the law? See Galatians 3:24.

_____

_____

7/What conclusions does he come to about himself (verses 14-24)? What is the predominant pronoun in these verses? What tension is Paul forced to face? How can you learn to deal with this same tension in your own life? Discuss this after reading Galatians 5:16-25.

_____

_____

_____

8/What hope is found in verse 25 for the miserable predicament of verse 24?

_____

_____

9/This chapter underscores the importance of union and identification with Christ. What steps have you, personally, taken to move out of bondage and into the freedom of life in Christ?

_____

_____

_____

CONCLUSION

It is not enough to be sincere and earnest in our fight with personal failure and sin. It is not even enough to be determined. We must rely on a power greater than the power of sin, greater than our own power. The way is not through self-effort. It is not a principle, but a _Person._ Pray about your own tendency to trust in self-effort more than in Jesus Christ. Thank God for the promise of deliverance in Christ.

7

ALIVE IN THE SPIRIT

ROMANS 8:1-17

Remember that this letter, as originally written, was not divided into chapters and verses. Here Paul simply continues to develop his major theme about God making men right with himself. Chapter 6 gave the secret to living the Christian life—life in Christ. Chapter 7 showed the bleakness of self-effort. Chapter 8 continues to explore what life in Christ is all about. No mention has been made of the Holy Spirit in Chapter 7, but he is the pervading power of Chapter 8, and "with his entry there is no further talk of defeat" (F. F. Bruce).

Romans 8:1-17

Read these verses aloud.
1/List the descriptive statements made in these verses about those who have the Holy Spirit living within them.

_____

_____

_____

_____

_____

note: If condemnation *(verse 1) were simply the opposite of* justification, *Paul would be saying now that those who are in Christ Jesus are justified; but that stage in the argument was reached back in 3:21 ff. The word for condemnation used in verse 1 means "the punishment following sentence— in other words,* penal servitude. *There is no reason why those who are in* Christ Jesus *should go on doing penal servitude as though they had never been pardoned and . . . liberated from the prison-house of sin"* (F. F. Bruce, Romans, *Eerdmans, p. 159).*

2/Contrast your list of Question 1 with what you know to be true of those who are controlled by their own sinful nature rather than by the Spirit of God. Can you validate the truths of these contrasts from your own experience? (Compare 2 Timothy 1:7.)

_____

_____

_____

_____

_____

3/In Romans 7:12, Paul describes the law as holy, righteous and good. How have the requirements of this righteous law been met (verses 3, 4)? Why is this essential? (Compare 3:25, 26.)

_____

_____

note: God did not change the law; he is changing us.

4/From reading verses 10 and 11, what do you conclude about the importance of our physical bodies? (Compare 1 Corinthians 6:14, 15, 19, 20; 2 Corinthians 4:14; 1 Thessalonians 4:14; 2 Corinthians 5:1-5.) What do these verses say about the wholeness of our salvation?

_____

_____

_____

5/What is the obligation for those who possess the Spirit of God (verses 12-15)? In your own words, state what God expects of his children. Compare Galatians 5:16; Romans 13:14.

_____

_____

_____

note: "Those who live by the Spirit, as Paul says, produce the fruit of the Spirit. A vine does not produce grapes by Act of Parliament; they are the fruit of the vine's own life; so the conduct which conforms to the standard of the Kingdom is not produced by any demand, not even God's, but it is the fruit of that divine nature which God gives as the result of what he has done in and by Christ" (F. F. Bruce, Romans, p. 163).

6/Can you know for sure that you are a Christian? How (verses 14-16)?

_____

note: The English equivalent of Abba would be Daddy, indicative of a close and loving relationship. Who dares to come this near to God? See Mark 14:36 and Galatians 4:6.

7/What special position do we have as God's own children? On what condition (verse 17b)? How does this increase our identification with Christ?

_____

_____

note: "Suffering now, glory hereafter" is a recurring theme in the New Testament and one that corresponds to the realities of life in the early Church. (Compare Acts 14:22; 2 Timothy 2:12; 1 Peter 1:6.)

8/Do believers today experience the conditions of 17b? Do you? What is the glory to be shared? How sure is it (John 17:24; Ephesians 1:13, 14)?

_____

_____

CONCLUSION

The crisis of what is called the conversion of John Wesley came when, in his words, he "exchanged the faith of a servant for the faith of a son."
Discuss how the above quotation applies to what you have just studied.

> To run and work the law commands,
> Yet gives me neither feet nor hands;
> But better news the Gospel brings:
> It bids me fly, and gives me wings.
> (quoted by F. F. Bruce, Romans, p. 162)

Close with prayer, thanking God for the liberty and family position given by Christ and asking for more understanding and experience of the privileges which are yours as children of God.

8

THE CHRISTIAN'S FORWARD LOOK

ROMANS 8:18-39

Paul has just written in verse 17 that we share in Christ's suffering in order that we may also share in his glory. We can almost see him pause here, remembering, and perhaps re-living, some of his own past problems as a Christian. Paul had paid a heavy price for being a disciple, a faithful apostle. As he reflects, he is caught up with the larger picture of life—not just the suffering but the anticipation of a glorious future.

Dr. William G. Coltman once said about this passage, "If you want to breathe the exhilarating air of assurance and confidence in the stuffy atmosphere of this world's chaos and uncertainty, then camp here and get your spiritual lungs filled. Standing on this lofty height the Apostle Paul let his eye sweep the future. The providence of God is the subject of his superlative persuasion."

Romans 8:18-27

Read these verses aloud from your usual translation. Then read them again in the the J. B. Phillips paraphrase of the New Testament.

1/Paul compares present suffering with future glory. What are some of the vivid contrasts of this passage? From 2 Corinthians 4:17, note what he had written to the Corinthians a year or two previously. How will all of creation be affected by our redemption? How does this make you feel? In verse 21, what do you think is included in "the glorious freedom of the children of God?"

_____

_____

_____

_____

_____

note: The "adoption as sons" here is the full manifestation of the believers' status as sons of God (compare verses 14, 15) —their entry upon the inheritance which is theirs by virtue of that status. (F. F. Bruce, Romans, p. 174)

2/Compare verse 23 with verse 11. In what sense can we say that we have the first fruits of the Spirit? What promise is there in the first "pickings" of an apple tree? Apply this to the question above. (Compare with Ephesians 1:13, 14.)

_____

_____

3/List some descriptive words and phrases by which you could characterize Paul's attitude toward life in verses 18-25. Read aloud and compare Romans 8:24, 25; 5:5; 1 Corinthians 4:18 and Hebrews 11:1, to find a definition of Christian hope. What is the biblical balance between the extremes of pessimism and optimistic fantasy? Has faith changed your attitude toward life? How?

_____

_____

_____

_____

4/Verse 26 starts out with the phrase "in the same way" or "likewise." To what previous idea does this refer? What do verses 26 and 27 teach you about prayer, and about God's response to our inadequacy? How deeply does God desire our prayers? What encouragement, during trials or inner heaviness, do you find in this work of the Spirit? Do you feel comforted at the thought of a "searched out" heart? Why?

_____

_____

_____

_____

5/As you look back over verses 1-27, review all the aspects of the Holy Spirit's ministry in a believer's life.

_____

_____

_____

Romans 8:28-39

Read these verses aloud.
6/In the face of these troubles, how does the over-ruling grace of God work on behalf of believers? Give an example from your own life. For what purpose (verse 29) has God called us, as believers? Note his long-range purpose in verse 30.

_____

_____

_____

7/Where does our salvation begin and end? When we are glorified, what will happen to us?

_____

_____

note: Verse 29—"The first-born of many brothers"—God's ultimate goal is to make us like Jesus, our "older brother."

Verse 30—A mystery surrounds each phase of this verse. That we are justi-fied is as much a mystery as our predestination. That God finally brings us to share his glory is the greatest mystery of all. Rather than engage in hair-splitting arguments about predestination and free will, we should fall on our faces and worship our gracious God. Even though we are redeemed, it is presumptuous for us to think that we should be able to understand fully all of the mysteries of God's ways.

8/What causes for anxiety might those believers be facing (verses 31-34)? Reword each of Paul's questions in the form of a positive statement. How is each statement a proof of the great love God has for us, in Christ?

_____

48

_____

_____

9/Read verse 31 with verse 28. How might this view of God differ from the concept of deity common among Roman pagans? How is verse 32 a demonstration of the principle stated in verse 28? What would you like to see included in the "all things?"

_____

_____

_____

10/What areas of life do the trials and afflictions of verses 35-39 cover?

_____

_____

note: Copy verse 32 and place it were you will see it often. Memorize and meditate on it often during the next week. Make it the basis of your prayers of worship and petition.

CONCLUSION
This study has caught us up in the great purpose of God's grace in bringing us into his family to share his glory. Think of it! God has called us to likeness to his Son, Jesus! Thank him that he has no lesser goal. Thank him for his love. Ask him to touch the deep places of your life with the security of the love of God in Christ Jesus.

> Jesus Christ, our sure foundation,
> He whose purpose stays the same,
> Building for himself a nation,
> Giving those he calls his name.
> Praise we now and evermore,
> Jesus, we adore!
> God has giv'n to us salvation,
> Jesus Christ has borne our blame.
> _Mark Hunt_

PAUL AND HIS KINSMEN

ROMANS 9 AND 10

Chapters 9-11 form what seems to the modern reader like a parenthesis, even a tangent. Chapter 8 ends with a resounding note of triumph in the love of Christ Jesus. What more can be said, we feel, except to urge readers to live as befits those who are indwelt by the Spirit, heirs to glory, loved and provided for by God himself? Thus, the opening verse of Chapter 12 seems like the next logical statement for Paul to make.

But Paul was a Jew, burdened for his own people. In these three chapters he wrestles with the problems peculiar to the Jews. How can Abraham's children fail to see that the way to righteousness is by faith in Christ? Indeed, the reader can almost feel Paul's pain as he grieves that many of his kinsmen are rejecting everything that he has just finished writing about!

Romans 9:1-29

Read these verses aloud.
1/How does Paul express the depth of his concern for his brothers? Compare Paul's attitude with that of Moses in Exodus 32:32. Have you ever felt the same kind of deep concern for your family and friends?

_____

_____

_____

2/From verses 4 and 5, list the eight advantages of having a Jewish heritage. How important was each of these factors? What did the Jews know about God?

_____

_____

_____

_____

note: It is one thing to spurn God's law; it is quite another thing to spurn his love. Read Jesus' view of this from Luke 20:9-18.

3/Paul uses examples from the Jews' own history to describe God's initiative of love and the Jews' responses. What major points does he make in verses 6-18? Who are Abraham's true children? Why did God tolerate Pharaoh's obstinacy for so long? What do we learn here about God's sovereignty?

_____

_____

_____

_____

4/In verse 19 Paul anticipates a very natural question. What is it and how does he answer it? What are God's "rights?" In what ways do people (you) question God? How does your understanding of the character of God determine the tone of your questioning? What, in turn, does the tone of your questions reveal about how well you know him?

_____

_____

_____

5/Because we have all failed (Romans 3:23), God has every right to punish and destroy us. What keeps him from doing it? What conclusions can you draw about God from verses 19-26? What is your personal response?

_____

_____

_____

note: As William Barclay explains in his commentary on Romans, p. 131, it is *impossible to think of the relationship between God and men simply in terms of justice. Man has no claim whatever on God. (The created has no claim on the Creator). Though men may appeal to justice, the answer is that man deserves nothing and can claim nothing from God. In God's dealings with men, the essential things are his will and his mercy.*

note: "It may be granted that the analogy of a potter and his pots covers only one aspect of the Creator's relation to those whom he has created, especially those whom he created in his own image. . . . Men, just because they are made in the image of God, insist on answering back. But there are different ways of answering him back. There is the answering back of faith, as when a Job or a Jeremiah call out for an account of God's mysterious ways with him. . . . There is, on the other hand, the answering back of unbelief and disobedience, when man tries to put God in the dock and sit in judgment upon him" (F. F. Bruce, Romans, p. 189).

Romans 9:30—10:13

Read these verses aloud.

6/Contrast the believing Gentiles' view of righteousness with that of the Jews. What "stone" caused the Jews to stumble? Why? (Notice the pronoun in the last phrase of Romans 9:33.) Why was this no problem for the Gentiles who believed? Discuss the implications of this problem of having preconceived ideas in your own friendships.

7/Read 10:4 in several translations. How *is* the law fulfilled? With what result? Read Philippians 3:4-6 in connection with Romans 10:2 in order to realize why Paul empathized with the Jews' problem of misdirected zeal.

8/What is the basic problem with righteousness through law-keeping in verse 5? Contrast this with the righteousness that comes through faith in verses 6-13. Is God ever partial or prejudiced? Who *can* be saved?

9/God took the initiative in our salvation, providing for all our needs in Jesus Christ. What are some of the elements of our response to him (verses 9-13)? Verses 9 and 10 have been called the first Christian creed. Do you believe in its major points? Have you acted upon your belief? How? What can you say about yourself in relation to God?

_____

_____

_____

_____

_____

_____

Romans 10:14-21

Read these verses aloud around the group.
10/Verse 13 naturally raises the questions of verses 14 and 15. How well do they express Paul's missionary concern? What is necessary in order for needy people to hear the message? How does this challenge you?

_____

_____

11/What opportunities has Israel had? Is there any excuse for their unbelief? If not, of what are they guilty? What further opportunity still awaits them? Draw your own word picture of the Lord from verse 21.

_____

_____

_____

_____

12/Quickly scan Chapters 9 and 10 again. What are their key verses?

_____

_____

_____

_____

_____

CONCLUSION

Have you experienced the kind of concern felt by Paul in 9:1-3 and 10:1? What view of God do you think needs to be shared with people you know? The answer to these two questions should bring to mind some fruitful ideas for closing the gap between your friends and God. Center your prayers around these thoughts as you close.

10

THE REMNANT

ROMANS 11

In concluding the discussion about his own people, the Jews, Paul asks two questions: *Did God reject his people? Did they stumble and fall beyond recovery?* His answer inspires a song of praise. God's mercy overwhelms us! All of salvation begins and ends in God himself.

For a review of Paul's argument about the Jews, re-read the questions he has asked in Chapters 9 and 10 (9:14, 19, 20, 22, 23; 10:14-16).

Romans 11:1-12

Read these verses aloud.

1/What is Paul's first proof that God has not rejected his chosen people? His second argument is from Jewish history. The story is found in 1 Kings 19:10, 14, 18. How did Elijah view the situation? What was God's reply to him? What is Paul's conclusion (verses 5, 6)?

_____

_____

_____

2/How do people enter the kingdom of God—by race, birth, inheritance, personal faith? as nations or as individuals? The United States is considered a Christian nation by other countries. How would you respond to such a statement?

_____

_____

3/In verse 7, the word translated "hardened" means "calloused." How does a callus develop? How sensitive to heat or pain is the skin that is calloused? What spiritual attitude does this illustrate?

_____

_____

_____

4/Verses 9 and 10 draw a picture for us of men sitting at a banquet table, feasting, unaware of danger. How does this illustrate the Jewish attitude to reality and truth?

_____

5/How will God's grace to the Gentiles affect Israel?

_____

Romans 11:13-24

Read these verses aloud.
6/How does Paul describe the effect of his own ministry to the Gentiles (verses 13, 14)? What is his hope? What two metaphors does Paul use to show that the Jews are not excluded from salvation (verse 16)? Re-phrase Paul's reasoning in your own words.

_____

_____

_____

note: The dough illustration comes from Numbers 15:17-21, where the Israelites were instructed to offer the first portion of their grain as a cake to the Lord, thus consecrating the whole harvest. God chose Abraham and set him apart. From Abraham sprang the whole Hebrew nation; and just as the whole harvest is consecrated by the offering of dough, or as the whole tree is consecrated when the root is holy, so the whole nation entered into a special relationship with God through Abraham. Thus Paul addresses a warning to Gentile believers not to despise the Jews, even in their rejection of Christ.

7/In verses 17-24, Paul further develops the analogy of the olive tree begun in verse 16b. Who is represented by the wild olive shoot? How is it nourished? What does this mean? What warning and what encouragement does Paul give? What action results in severity from God? In kindness? What is the only basis of life and healthy growth for both natural and grafted-in branches (verse 20)?

_____   _____

_____

_____

_____

Romans 11:25-36

Read these verses aloud.
8/What is Israel's future hope (verse 26)? Through whom will this be accomplished? Describe in your own words Israel's present position, according to verse 28.

_____

_____

_____

note: Israel refers to the descendents of Jacob, whose name was changed to Israel (Genesis 32:27, 28). Biblical scholars differ as to whether it refers to the political nation of Israel as it now exists.

Verse 32: "Mercy on all" means all without distinction rather than all without exception.

9/The thought of God's mercy launches Paul into a song of praise. What truths about God can you discover in this doxology?

_____

_____

_____

CONCLUSION
Verses 33-36 are the climax to all that Paul has written about both Jews and Gentiles in Chapters 9-11. We have observed, with him, the display of God's mercy in planning and unfolding the panorama of salvation. He began with one chosen man, Abraham, the first Jew, to whom he committed truth about himself and from whom he formed a nation. The Jews became the recipients and guardians of the knowledge of God, and from among them was born the

Savior of the world—Jesus, a fulfillment of God's promise to Abraham, "Through you shall all the families of the earth be blessed" (Genesis 12:3).

God's plan has never been thwarted, not even when Abraham's descendents rebelled and then rejected the Messiah. God continues to pour his blessing on any Jew, any Gentile, who responds to him in faith and obedience by calling "on the name of the Lord" (10:13). We are blessed as we join and live among that body of true believers.

Let Paul's doxology draw you into praising and thanking God for his mercy, as you close this Bible study session.

11

LIVING THE CHRISTIAN LIFE

ROMANS 12

Justified, reconciled, indwelt by the Holy Spirit, adopted into God's family —how then should we live? Our new standing with God should radically affect our lifestyle and our relationships. Paul's teaching in this chapter reminds us of Jesus' Sermon on the Mount; here, in Paul's energetic style, is a description of what the Christian life is all about.

Romans 12:1-8

Read these verses aloud.
1/What dramatic, practical action does Paul urge believers to take? What is the basis of his appeal? Why should anyone offer himself to God in this way?

_____

_____

_____

2/What is the significance of offering our bodies to God? Why not just our souls? Who is our chief example of this (Hebrews 10:5-7)? What are the implications of being a *living* sacrifice? How does God view such a sacrifice on the part of believers?

_____

_____

_____

note: *"True worship is the offering to God of one's body, and all that one does with it every day" (Barclay,* Romans, *p. 157).*

3/Some people are spiritual chameleons in their contact with the world. What is the problem with this? (If you don't know what a chameleon is, check your dictionary!) From verse 2, describe the Christian mind-set. Why do you think Paul emphasizes the mind rather than the spirit, in verse 2? How may we *prove* the will of God? How is his will described?

_____

_____

_____

_____

note: J. B. Phillips translates verse 2: "Don't let the world around you squeeze you into its own mold, but let God re-mold your minds from within, so that you may prove in practice that the plan of God for you is good, meets all his demands and moves towards the goal of true maturity."

4/How are believers to evaluate themselves? Why (verses 3-8)? What should we learn about ourselves? What should be our view of others? How should this affect our tendency to compare ourselves with others? What happens when we refuse to recognize our own gifts and covet someone else's?

_____

_____

_____

_____

note: Diversity, not uniformity, is the mark of God's handiwork. It is so in nature; it is so in grace, too, and nowhere more than in the Christian community" (F. F. Bruce, Romans, p. 227).

5/List the gifts in verses 6-8. Is any individual gift given more importance than others? What is important about us and our gifts? How do you know what your gift is? Where did it come from? Think and pray how God would have you use your gift(s) this week.

_____

_____

_____

Romans 12:9-13

Read these verses aloud.

6/List Paul's rules for daily Christian living. To view these rules freshly, try changing each to its opposite (e.g. "Let love be hypocritical."), and contrast the changed quality of life resulting in each instance.

_____

_____

_____

_____

_____

_____

7/Discuss each rule individually, noticing the different verbs used. With what attitude is each of these rules to be obeyed? Should a Christian be a pessimist? Explain. Share how the Holy Spirit has tugged at your life to conform you to these rules.

_____

_____

_____

_____

_____

_____

note: Verse 13—"The Christian is to be given to hospitality. Over and over again the New Testament insists on this duty of the open door. (See Hebrews 13:2, I Timothy 3:2, Titus 1:8, I Peter 4:9.) Tyndale used a magnificent word when he translated it that the Christian should have a harborous disposition. A home can never be happy when it is selfish. Christianity is the religion of the open hand, the open heart and the open door" (Barclay, Romans, p. 167).

Romans 12:14-21

Read these verses aloud.

8/What further principles does Paul give for living in a tough world? Again, change each into its opposite and note the change in the quality of life; try to imagine a world in which none of these principles was ever lived out. Give examples from the life of Christ that demonstrate how he fulfilled these principles. What are *your* resources for relating to others like this?

_____

_____

_____

_____

_____

_____

note: J. B. Phillips translates verse 21: "Don't allow yourself to be overpowered by evil. Take the offensive—overpower evil with good!"

9/Look back over the chapter. Write a brief title for each paragraph and note the lesson to be learned.

	title	*lesson to be learned*
Verses 1, 2	_____	_____
Verses 3-8	_____	_____
Verses 9-13	_____	_____
Verses 14-21	_____	_____

10/Which exhortations have been neglected in your life? Which would you like to see springing into life in you, by the power of God's Spirit? Share them with the group.

CONCLUSION
Each of you volunteer to pray for another person in the group so that each is remembered in prayer before God. Pray especially and specifically for the needs expressed in the last question.

12

CHRISTIAN RESPONSIBILITY

ROMANS 13

The Jews had a reputation as a rebellious people. The zealots, in particular, were not content with passive resistance against Rome, and their acts of terrorism and insurrection plagued Roman governors. Jesus' enemies tried to identify him with this group when they wanted the Romans to crucify Christ; and in the early days of Christianity, the Romans tended to identify Christians as a Jewish sect, because most of the Christian church consisted of Jewish believers.

However, the Roman Empire allowed its subject nations remarkable freedom. As a result, Jewish religious practices were carefully safeguarded, regardless of how superstitious and absurd they might have seemed to the Romans. For instance, Imperial order forbade the carrying of military standards with images into the holy city of Jerusalem because of the Jewish prohibition against "graven images." The Romans also had a reputation for justice. (Paul appealed to Rome for judicial rights in Acts 22:25.) Yet even when Emperors Nero and Domitian began to persecute the church, the words of Paul and Peter continued to guide Christians into submission to the governing powers.

Romans 13

Read the whole chapter aloud around the group.
1/Divide the chapter into three paragraphs, assigning to each a subject title. (Entitling the paragraphs helps you to get a handle on the whole chapter, an idea you might want to use when you study other Bible passages.)

_____

_____

_____

2/Discuss the following questions: What do verses 1-7 teach about authority? About rulers? About obedience? About taxes? About respect?

_____

_____

_____

_____

_____

3/The importance of this teaching to Christians is emphasized by its repetition in 1 Timothy 2:1, 2; Titus 3:1 and 1 Peter 2:13-17. Christ's kingship and his kingdom were often misunderstood. (Read John 19:14-19 and Acts 17:6-8.) What corrective is given by the teaching of Romans 13? Do people still misunderstand the kingship of Jesus? Is it possible for us as believers to reconcile the truth of his kingship with the reality of the other authority figures in our lives—of government, school, family or business? How?

_____

_____

_____

_____

_____

4/Is civil disobedience ever appropriate? What should we do when "Caesar" claims not only the things that are his, but the things that are God's (Matthew 22:17-21; Acts 5:29)? How does Christian obedience to authority make Christian protest more powerful?

_____

_____

_____

5/Should we ever dissociate ourselves from the society in which we live? What does the state or government do for each of us?

_____

6/According to verse 7, what do we owe the state in which we live? What is our private debt (verses 8-10)? When is this debt paid off?

7/In what one rule are all the commandments listed in verse 9 fulfilled? (Compare also Galatians 5:14; James 2:8.) Who is your neighbor? To what degree are we to love our neighbor? How will low self-esteem in us affect our love of our neighbor?

8/What does Paul anticipate when he calls believers to be alert (verse 11)? What is the salvation that is "nearer now?" Compare I Peter 1:5; Romans 8:23 and Hebrews 9:28.

9/Paul contrasts night and day. What does this metaphor illustrate? What does the light reveal? Does this frighten or comfort you? Discuss how light can be "armor" (verse 12b). How should the nearness of the "day" affect our life style? Compare 1 Thessalonians 5:4-9.

10/What observations can you make about the behavior described in verse 13, 14b?

11/The word "but" signifies a contrast. In practical terms, what does it mean to you to clothe yourself with the Lord Jesus Christ—to "put on" Christ? Compare Ephesians 4:24, Colossians 3:12.

note: Verses 13 and 14 were the turning point in the life of Augustine. He sat weeping in the garden of a friend, almost persuaded to begin a new life and be done with the old life of immoral living. He was in despair about his inability to do either when he heard a child singing in a neighboring house, "Take up and read! Take up and read!" Taking up the scroll that lay at his friend's side, his eyes fell on the words of Romans 13:13, 14. "No further would I read, nor had I any need; instantly at the end of this sentence, a clear light flooded my heart and all the darkness of doubt vanished away." (Augustine, Confessions, 8.29).

CONCLUSION

The three paragraphs of this chapter provide three subjects for prayer: a) your responsibility to authorities, b) your responsibility to others, c) your responsibility to live thoughtfully, aware of the shortness of life.

Be honest and practical as you pray together—praying for national and local leaders by name, for those you need to love more carefully and consistently and for your own "clothing" awareness.

13

THE STRONG AND THE WEAK

ROMANS 14—15:3

Christian liberty walks a narrow path between legalism and license. Paul knew from his own background how easy it is to add legalistic requirements to God's liberating truths. Yet Paul grew to become the most liberated of believers. F. F. Bruce writes about Paul's freedom, "So completely emancipated was he from spiritual bondage that he was not even in bondage to his emancipation." In this chapter, Paul warns us against a judgmental spirit toward others who may not have grown to the same level of freedom that we have.

Romans 14:1-12

Read these verses aloud.
1/Two kinds of faith are being discussed in verses 1-6. How would you characterize each? What two specific issues have arisen as a cause for disagreement among believers? How crucial are they in terms of Christian living? In contrast, what are some issues in the Christian life about which we must feel deep conviction, not merely personal scruples?

_____

_____

_____

_____

2/Give possible reasons why a person may be weak in faith. Compare Galatians 4:8-11 and Colossians 2:16, 17.

_____

_____

3/How should we relate to those whose definition of Christian freedom differs from ours? Why? What happens when we push our personal scruples onto others? What principles should govern your decisions about how you behave? How can you discern the difference between scruples that are dictated by convention (or superstition) and those that are the result of conviction? Give examples from your own experience.

_____

_____

_____

_____

4/Express verses 7 and 8 in your own words. What do *all* Christians have in common? Why should this be the point of emphasis rather than personal lifestyle? Who is central in both life and death for the Christian?

_____

_____

_____

_____

5/From verses 10-12, who has the right to judge anyone? What should be our posture before this judge? Why is outspoken criticism or disdain of our brothers in these matters inappropriate? What is its effect on the community of believers?

_____

_____

_____

_____

Romans 14:13-23

Read these verses aloud.
6/What voluntary limits should shape our freedom (verses 13-15)? What principle about uncleanness helps us to understand our own scruples and others' (verse 14)? Remind yourself of the Jewish dietary prohibitions (for

example, Deuteronomy 14:1-21) and *sense* how offensive it would be to be served prohibited food. Now imagine what an issue like this would mean in the early church with its mixture of Jewish and Gentile believers. Compare I Corinthians 8:4-13; 10:23-33.

_____

_____

_____

_____

_____

7/How does Paul's reminder in verse 17 set things in true perspective? Discuss how the three descriptive words about God's kingdom should affect our willingness to forego some pleasure for the sake of another. If we have hurt a brother, can we have "joy in the Holy Spirit?"

_____

_____

8/Why would Paul allow the person with the weaker faith to dictate his actions? Why is mutual edification (verse 19) important? What clearcut principles for action do you find in verses 19-23 for the person who is strong in faith? For the person whose faith is weak?

_____

_____

_____

_____

Romans 15:1-13

Read these verses aloud.
9/Who is our example for personal behavior? What freedoms were his? Christ has accepted you. How should this help you to accept others? How can we guard against laxity or lowered standards in our acceptance of others?

_____

10/Whom should you please (verse 1)? Discuss. In what four ways do the Scriptures help us? What does God's steadfastness and encouragement enable us to do (verses 5-7)?

11/To underscore the teaching of verse 7, Paul summarizes God's plan for mankind. Remember, this was written to a group of new believers composed of two peoples who had never mixed—Jews and Gentiles. Read verse 8 in several translations. What is Paul's logic here? What is predicted in the four Old Testament passages quoted (verses 9-12)? What is the mood of these prophecies?

12/How is God described in verse 13? Why is hope so important in this discussion? What does God give us? How does it become ours?

CONCLUSION

After analyzing your own faith (strong or weak) ask yourself, "How willing am I to give up something I enjoy for the good of someone else?" And are you overflowing with hope that God will make the changes you know are necessary in your own life and others' lives? The answers to these questions will give you plenty to pray about. Make your prayers short and specific and close with verse 13 as a benediction.

14

A GLIMPSE OF THE EARLY CHURCH

ROMANS 15:14—16:27

Paul closes his letter to the Romans with a personal word about his ministry and his hopes for the future. From the list of greetings to individuals in Chapter 16—people he has met elsewhere who now live in Rome—we sense the vibrancy of the first century church. We can only speculate what exciting stories lie behind each name! Paul includes a brief apostolic warning, gives a call to prayer, then closes this great letter with a benediction full of praise to God.

Romans 15:14-33

Read these verses aloud.
1/How did Paul regard those to whom he is writing? How did he view his ministry? Its extent? Its strategy? What was his priestly duty? For what purpose? Of what did his witness consist (verse 18)? How is this a good pattern for our own personal witness?

_____

_____

_____

_____

2/What were Paul's future plans? Why was he going to Jerusalem? What practical teaching does he include (verses 26, 27)? From your own experience, what does giving do for the one who gives? The one who receives? Their unity?

_____

_____

_____

3/Why do you think Paul felt the need for partners (verse 30)? In what future activities did he need prayer support? What dangers did he fear? Read Acts 21:17-20, 27-35 ff. to discover what happened.

_____

_____

Romans 16

Read these verses aloud. (Be sure to assign the reading to someone who can handle the "foreign" names in this passage!)
4/Who was Phoebe? Where was she going? What were her credentials? What did Paul request for her? Note how this exemplifies his teaching in 12:13.

_____

_____

5/What kind of people were Prisca and Aquila? See Acts 18:2, 3, 18, 24-26.

_____

_____

6/What facts do you learn about the life of the early church from the descriptions of individuals in verses 3-16? How many of the greetings go to women? From the descriptive phrases repeated in this listing, what characterized members of this early church? With what descriptive phrase would you like to hear *your* life summed up?

_____

_____

_____

7/What two kinds of trouble-makers does Paul warn about in verses 17, 18? What is his concern in verse 19? Compare Matthew 10:16 or 1 Corinthians 14:20. What is the ultimate end of evil?

_____

_____

8/What individuals add their greetings to those of Paul (verses 21-24)? What do you know about them?

_____

_____

9/In the benediction (verses 25-27), list at least six things you learn about the Gospel.

_____

_____

_____

CONCLUSION
In the book of *Romans* you have read and discussed the most profound truths to be found in the Bible. Because of their depth and complexity, some of these teachings may still seem difficult for you to get a "handle" on. As long as a truth remains abstract it will seem to be beyond your grasp. But ask the Holy Spirit to grip your heart and life with these ideas of Paul. As they are translated into practical reality in your relationship with God and with others, you will come to understand and experience these truths more clearly and intimately. As you *live* your faith you will learn to put Paul's doctrines to work.

As a review of the central themes of *Romans,* look back over each section and assign to it a one-sentence title to remind you of its content. This will help you to be a good steward of the truth in this letter from Paul.

Romans 1 _____

2—3:20 _____

3:21—4 _____

5 _____

6 _____

7 _____

74

8:1-17 _____

8:18-39 _____

9, 10 _____

11 _____

12 _____

13 _____

14:1—15:13 _____

15:14—16 _____

On the personal level: What has changed in you since you first started this study of *Romans?* Record below any personal resolutions, decisions, fresh commitments or new understanding. Expressing and recording such changes will help you to consolidate the gains in your spiritual growth.

_____

_____

_____

_____

_____

_____

BIBLIOGRAPHY

Barclay, William. *The Letter to the Romans* (Daily Bible Study Series), Philadelphia: Westminster Press, 1955.

Bruce, F. F. *The Epistle of Paul to the Romans* (Tyndale New Testament Commentaries), Grand Rapids: Wm. B. Eerdmans Publishing Company, 1963.

RECOMMENDED SUPPLEMENTARY READING

Stott, John R. W. *Men Made New* (An exposition of Romans 5-8), Chicago: Inter-Varsity Press, 1966.

Lloyd-Jones, Martyn D. *Romans,* Grand Rapids: Zondervan Publishing House, 1975.

WHAT NEXT?

If you're like most Bible study groups, your question now is, "What shall we study next?"

To help you with that question, we've developed the chart below so that you can find your own level and area of interest. If this particular studyguide matches the pace and depth of analysis that your group needs, chances are that other Fisherman studyguides in the same level will be right for you as well. Simply pick one of the many studyguides that are available at your appropriate level.

Later On

When you finish your next studyguide, we recommend that you move on *in a sequence* by selecting from either another subject area or a different level. Continue in order from there. Many Bible study groups have a high degree of cohesiveness that extends over a period of time. By using studyguides in sequence you will:

   a. Grow in maturity as a group,

   b. Cover the major areas of Christian life and belief in a systematic and balanced manner,

   c. Learn to study God's Word in depth through the inductive method.

	Learning about God	Personal growth in Christ	Living out our faith
Level 1 *Beginning*	Mark Ecclesiastes David: Vol. I	Proverbs and Parables Higher Ground Psalms	Acts 1-12 Letters to the Thessalonians The Church
Level 2 *Inter-mediate*	Genesis 1-25 John David: Vol. II	Genesis 25-50 James Philippians Guidance and God's Will	Acts 13-28 Building Your House on the Lord Ephesians
Level 3 *Advanced*	Romans Hebrews	The God Who Understands Me 1 Corinthians Let's Pray Together	Amos Letters to Timothy Revelation

Available at your local bookstore or from:
Harold Shaw Publishers, Box 567, Wheaton, IL 60187